DATE DUE

WESTWOOD JUNIOR HIGH SCHOOL

19432

CLASSIFIED; SPIES   327
Hyde, Natalie.

CLASSIFIED: SPIES AT WORK

Natalie Hyde

JL BANTE
DOLD
FREDERICK

PH EBELING
RICHARD EICHENLAUB
HEINRICH CARL EILERS
PAUL FEHSE
EDMUND CARL HEINE
FELIX JA

E KAERCHER
JOSEF KLEIN
HARTWIG KLEISS
HERMAN LANG
EVELYN CLAYTON LEWIS
RENE EMANUEL

L REUPER
EVERETT ROEDER
PAUL SCHOLZ
GEORGE GOTTLOB SCHUH
ERWIN WILHELM SIEGLER
OSCAR ST

H STADE
LILLY STEIN
FRANZ JOSEPH STIGLER
ERICK STRUNK
LEO WAALEN
ADOLF WALIS

USTENFELD
AXEL WHEELER-HILL
BERTRAM W. ZENZINGER

THE
33 CONVICTED MEMBERS
OF THE
DUQUESNE
SPY RING

Westmont Junior High School
Media Center
Westmont, IL 60559

CRABTREE
Publishing Company
www.crabtreebooks.com

Crabtree Publishing Company
www.crabtreebooks.com

Author: Natalie Hyde
**Publishing plan research
 and development**: Reagan Miller
Editors: Sonya Newland, Kathy Middleton
Proofreader: Wendy Scavuzzo
Photo Researcher: Sonya Newland
Original design: Tim Mayer
 (Mayer Media)
Book design: Tim Mayer
Cover design: Ken Wright
**Production coordinator and
 prepress tecnician**: Ken Wright
Print coordinator: Katherine Berti

Produced for Crabtree Publishing
Company by White-Thomson Publishing

Cover:
Wikimedia: (bottom right inset); Petr Novák:
(top left inset); **Shutterstock:** Galina Barskaya:
(center inset); SMA Studio: (left)

Photographs:
Corbis: Alex Milan Tracy/Demotix: p.
33; Bettmann: p. 34; Hulton-Deutsch
Collection: pp. 18–19; Roger Ressmeyer:
p. 13; Dreamstime: Basphoto: p. 14; Felix
Mizioznikov: p. 24; Igor Dolgov: p. 15t;
Getty: Popperfoto: pp. 40–41; Library of
Congress: pp. 1, 12, 25b; **Shutterstock:** Adam
Gregor: p. 17; Andrey_Popov: pp. 42–43;
ArtisticPhoto: p. 6; bertie: p. 37; BMCL: p. 35;
Bocman1973: p. 45; CRM: p. 27; iQoncept:
p. 16; Kiev.Victor: p. 31; Kzenon: p. 20;
Lightspring: p. 42; Master-L: p. 9; Nestor
Noci: p. 11; Nomad_Soul: p. 26; Paul Drabot:
pp. 22–23; Rommel Canlas: p. 7; ruskpp: p.
3; **Thinkstock:** Creatas: p. 25t; **Topfoto:** The
Granger Collection: pp. 4–5, 28; TopFoto/
ImageWorks: p. 8; Topham Picturepoint: pp.
38–39; **Wikimedia:** pp. 29, 30, 36; Espen Moe:
p. 44; Gary Blakeley: p. 21; Krimidoedel: p.
15b; vlasta2, bluefootedbooby on flickr.com:
p. 10; www.navy.mil: p. 32.

Library and Archives Canada Cataloguing in Publication

Hyde, Natalie, 1963-, author
 Classified : spies at work / Natalie Hyde.

(Crabtree chrome)
Includes index.
Issued in print and electronic formats.
ISBN 978-0-7787-1335-7 (bound).--ISBN 978-0-7787-1397-5 (pbk.).--
ISBN 978-1-4271-8978-3 (pdf).--ISBN 978-1-4271-8972-1 (html)

 1. Espionage--Juvenile literature. 2. Spies--Juvenile literature.
I. Title. II. Series: Crabtree chrome

UB270.5.H93 2014   j327.12   C2014-903913-1
                                           C2014-903914-X

Library of Congress Cataloging-in-Publication Data

CIP available at the Library of Congress

Crabtree Publishing Company
www.crabtreebooks.com   1-800-387-7650

Printed in the U.S.A./092014/JA20140811

Copyright © **2015 CRABTREE PUBLISHING COMPANY**. All rights reserved. No part of this publication may be
reproduced, stored in a retrieval system or be transmitted in any form or by any means, electronic, mechanical, photocopying,
recording, or otherwise, without the prior written permission of Crabtree Publishing Company. In Canada: We acknowledge
the financial support of the Government of Canada through the Canada Book Fund for our publishing activities.

Published in Canada
Crabtree Publishing
616 Welland Ave.
St. Catharines, ON
L2M 5V6

Published in the United States
Crabtree Publishing
PMB 59051
350 Fifth Avenue, 59th Floor
New York, New York 10118

Published in the United Kingdom
Crabtree Publishing
Maritime House
Basin Road North, Hove
BN41 1WR

Published in Australia
Crabtree Publishing
3 Charles Street
Coburg North
VIC 3058

Contents

Life in the Shadows

A Spy's Mission

New York had fallen to the British. Nathan Hale was a captain in the American Revolutionary War. His **mission** was to gather information on British troops. He knew that the penalty for spying was death. He crossed the river into New York in disguise. He asked questions and made notes.

A Light on the Water

Hale waited at the river on the day the boatman had agreed on for his return. When a boat appeared, he signaled with his light. He didn't realize that the boat belonged to the British. He was turned in by someone who had recognized him. The British found Hale's notes hidden in the soles of his shoes. This was all the evidence they needed to hang him.

◄ *Nathan Hale was only 21 when the British hanged him as a spy.*

> "I only regret that I have but one life to lose for my country."
>
> Nathan Hale

mission: an important job

Why Spy?

A spy is someone who secretly gathers **classified** information. Spies get details on the movements and plans of enemies. Then they have to deliver what they learned to the government they work for. It can be dangerous. If they are caught, it can cost them their lives.

▲ *Countries often switch from friends to enemies. In the 1700s, the United States saw the Soviet Union (Russia) as a great trading partner. During the Cold War, the two countries were bitter enemies (see page 36).*

What Do You Want to Know?

Countries spy on other countries to find out if there are threats to their security. They even spy on friendly nations. This way, they can be sure that they are keeping promises. They also know that sometimes friends can become enemies. If that happens, they are ready to protect their nation.

> "Though the enemy be stronger in numbers, we may prevent him from fighting. Scheme [make plans] so as to discover his plans and the likelihood of their success."
>
> from *The Art of War*, Sun Tzu

▶ *Spies fear arrest for the rest of their lives. Some have been caught up to 30 years after they stopped spying.*

classified: very secret and only available to authorized people

Industrial Spies

Sometimes companies hire spies to help their business. These spies try to steal formulas or plans for new products from competitors. This is called industrial **espionage**. Sometimes spies do not work for anyone. They spy for their own reasons. They might not trust the government. They might feel people have the right to know secret information.

▼ *Spanish business executive Jose Ignacio Lopez was in charge of buying auto parts for General Motors. He left GM in the 1990s to work for Volkswagen. GM accused him of stealing trade secrets and giving them to VW.*

▶ *Hackers are called 'white hat' or 'black hat.' White-hat hackers test security systems to find problems. Black-hat hackers break into databases or destroy data for fun.*

Computer Hackers

Spying is often done through computers. A lot of private information is stored there. People who figure out passwords and break into other computers are called hackers. They can learn where someone lives and works. They can also pry into bank accounts and steal credit card numbers. Some hackers do it for fun. Others sell the information.

An engineer with Gillette worked on a new razor design. He sold the secret drawings to other companies. He was caught and spent two years in prison.

espionage: spying to get information

9

Spying in History

As long as there has been war, there have been spies. Military leaders have always known that the key to winning is to know the enemy. Sun Tzu was a general in ancient China. In his book *The Art of War*, he explained how **vital** spies were to winning a war.

▲ *Sun Tzu wrote that there were five kinds of spies: local spies, internal spies, double spies, dead spies (enemy spies that spread false information for you), and living spies (survivors who bring information back on the enemy).*

"An army without spies is like a man without ears or eyes."

Chia Lin

Ancient Spies

Ramses II was an ancient Egyptian pharaoh. He was almost defeated by Hittite spies. They had spread lies about the location of their army. But Ramses didn't believe them. He brought in more troops and avoided disaster. The ancient Greeks, Romans, and even the Aztecs also used spies.

▲ *Ramses II is called "Ramses the Great." He managed to hold his power during many attacks on Egypt by outsmarting his enemies.*

vital: very necessary

The CIA

The Central Intelligence Agency (CIA) employs many agents, or spies. The United States government uses them to collect **restricted** information. Spying grew and changed during World War II. After the war, in 1947, the United States passed the National Security Act. It created a central spy agency. The CIA is the leading spy service in the world.

▼ *At the CIA headquarters, there is a museum full of secret spy gear. It is only open to special guests.*

▲ *The CIA holds daily meetings to study current events around the world and to plan operations.*

It can take more than two years to become a CIA agent. Even then, spies must pass a lie detector test every few years to keep their jobs.

The Canadian Security Intelligence Service (CSIS)

CSIS is Canada's spy agency. It collects and studies all kinds of data. Its headquarters are in Ottawa, Ontario. CSIS agents also work overseas. They talk to local people to gather information. With these reports, they can alert the government to any threats.

restricted: only available to certain people

Who Is Spying on Whom?

Britain's Secret Intelligence Service (SIS) is also known as MI6, which stands for Military Intelligence, Section 6. It was created in 1909. For almost 90 years, the government did not admit it even existed. The main target for MI6 after World War II was the **Soviet Union**. Spies for the Soviet agency, or the KGB, were known as some of the best at getting information. After the breakup of the Soviet Union in 1991, the KGB became the FSB in Russia.

▼ *The MI6 building is very well built. It even survived a missile attack in 2000.*

◀ *The Russian FSB includes the Federal Border Guards. They patrol land and sea looking for drug smugglers, terrorists, and other criminals.*

No Pictures, Please

The Inter-Services Intelligence (ISI) is the intelligence agency in Pakistan. It is one of the largest agencies in the world. Some believe the number of agents is around 10,000. They are so secret, the exact number is not known. None of their staff has ever been caught on camera.

John Le Carré is famous for writing spy novels. He was an MI6 agent himself. He changed his name from David Cromwell because agents weren't allowed to publish novels under their own names.

Soviet Union: a former Russian country made up of 15 states

▲ *Agencies look for people who are open to working in other countries and can speak other languages.*

So You Want to Be a Spy...

When agencies hire new spies, they look for people with special skills. They need people who stay calm under stress. They want people who have jobs where they can get their hands on information. People who speak other languages are very useful. Sometimes people apply to work for the agency. Sometimes the agency offers a job to a particular person.

What a Great Job

How in the world do agencies get people to take on a job with so much risk? They could lose their cover jobs. They could be arrested. They could even lose their lives. Many times they can't even tell their families what they are doing. Agencies argue that the risks are worth more than doing nothing to help.

When spies are hired, they are not told the names of other spies or **officials**. That is so that if they are ever caught, they can't put other people in danger.

officials: people with special duties

Double Trouble

Double agents are a problem for agencies. These are spies who pretend to work for one agency, while secretly working for another. Switching sides is called "turning." Some agents want to turn because they are unhappy with their group. Sometimes they are threatened with death if they don't turn.

Spy Rings

A spy ring is a group of spies working together. The Duquesne Spy Ring was the largest in U.S. history. During World War II, 33 German spies took jobs in the United States in airports and restaurants, and as delivery people. The ring was **exposed** by a double agent. The Portland Spy Ring was a group spying for Russia in England in the 1950s. One of them attracted too much attention by spending his money wildly. The group was discovered and arrested.

◀ *Ethel Gee served nine years in prison for her part in the Portland Spy Ring.*

A mole is a "sleeper agent." Moles work their way into an organization. Then they wait, sometimes years, until they get the order to act.

exposed: made known to the public

Spy Skills

Training Spies

To keep their names secret, spies often train outside their own country. Training to be a spy is very intense. They practice hand-to-hand combat. They learn survival methods. The use of weapons and martial arts are also a part of their training.

▲ *Martial arts training improves fitness, coordination, and focus.*

The Farm

Good agents also need other skills. They need to know how to find and collect evidence of threats to security. The CIA has a training center called "The Farm." It takes its nickname from Camp X, a famous World War II training center located on a farm in Ontario, Canada. British and American agents were trained there.

▶ *Some Camp X programs taught agents how to kill an enemy. It earned the nickname "the school of mayhem and murder."*

CAMP X
1941 – 1946

ON THIS SITE BRITISH SECURITY CO-ORDINATION OPERATED SPECIAL TRAINING SCHOOL No. 103 AND HYDRA.

S.T.S. 103 TRAINED ALLIED AGENTS IN THE TECHNIQUES OF SECRET WARFARE FOR THE SPECIAL OPERATIONS EXECUTIVE (S O E) BRANCH OF THE BRITISH INTELLIGENCE SERVICE.

HYDRA NETWORK COMMUNICATED VITAL MESSAGES BETWEEN CANADA, THE UNITED STATES AND GREAT BRITAIN.

THIS COMMEMORATION IS DEDICATED TO THE SERVICE OF THE MEN AND WOMEN WHO TOOK PART IN THESE OPERATIONS.

IN MEMORY OF
SIR WILLIAM STEPHENSON
"The Man Called Intrepid"
BORN AT WINNIPEG, MANITOBA, CANADA, JANUARY 11, 1896.
DIED AT PAGET, BERMUDA, JANUARY 31, 1989.
DIRECTOR OF BRITISH SECURITY CO-ORDINATION
1941-1946

Universities now give courses that train **cyber** spies. They learn how to hack into computers and crack passwords. They also find data and write viruses.

cyber: to do with computers

Surveillance

The most important job a spy has is to observe. Spies watch to find out where people go, when guards move, or where things are hidden. Powerful tools such as binoculars, telescopes, and **drones** let them see things from far away.

▶ *Cameras on board drones can clearly see objects the size of a milk carton from 60,000 feet (18,288 meters).*

I Can Hear You

Listening is another way to get information. A great skill is lip reading. This means the spy can "see" a conversation. Another way to hear is through bugs, which are tiny hidden microphones. They are so small that they can be placed almost anywhere.

During World War II, MI6 secretly taped German prisoners of war. They placed bugs in fireplaces, lamps, and even in the trees in the garden. They learned about a secret new German rocket that way.

drones: unmanned planes that are controlled from far away

Breaking In and Getting Out

Sometimes spies need to get into buildings, rooms, or safes. Picking locks is a skill they learn. Most spies know that it is easier to be let into a building than to have to break in. To get in the easy way, they may pretend to be someone else and use fake ID, or identification, cards.

▲ *Burglars tend to break windows to get in. Agents pick locks so no one will know they were there.*

◀ *In some places, you can go to prison for up to seven years for making fake ID cards.*

The Invisible Man

The best disguise for a spy is to look like everyone else around them. They learn how to blend in with their clothing and the way they act. Often, agencies will "plant" a spy in a job. This means they get them a job where they want information.

Fritz Duquesne was a Nazi spy. In prison, he faked being **paralyzed** for two years so he could stay in the prison hospital. There, he cut the bars on the window and jumped to freedom.

paralyzed: unable to move all or part of a person's body

Cracking Codes

Most important information is written in code so no one else can read it. Code breakers crack the codes so the message can be understood. Today, computers do most of the work. Some intelligence agencies put coded messages on their websites. People who are able to crack the code are invited to apply for jobs.

▲ *Most data that is sent over the Internet is written in code to keep it secure.*

Native American "code talkers" sent coded messages during both world wars. They used words from their native languages. The enemy couldn't crack the code.

Secret Weapons

The best weapons for spies are small and easily hidden. Guns can be made to look like belt buckles, pens, or cigarettes. Spy cameras can be as small as a thimble. They can be hidden in eyeglasses or brooches. **Microchips** can be as small as a dot and hidden anywhere.

▲ *Some mini cameras come with a built-in microphone as well.*

 microchips: tiny electronic devices that can perform many tasks

Elizabeth Van Lew

Elizabeth Van Lew was from a wealthy Quaker family in Virginia. During the American Civil War, Van Lew visited Union soldiers in prison and helped many escape. She and her ring of spies also gave reports on Confederate troops to Union officers. She carried coded messages inside eggshells and the soles of her shoes.

◀ *Elizabeth Van Lew was included in the Military Intelligence Hall of Fame in 1993 for her work in the Civil War.*

Mata Hari

Margaretha Zelle was born in the Netherlands. She ran off at age 18 to marry an army captain in the Dutch East Indies (now Indonesia). There she took up exotic dancing. After her divorce, she moved to Paris and performed under her stage name Mata Hari. She became a star and had relationships with powerful men. During World War I, she claimed to be a spy for the French. But the French arrested and **executed** her for being a spy for the Germans.

▶ *Secret ink was found in Mata Hari's room. This was supposedly evidence of her spying. She said it was part of her makeup.*

"**I am a woman who enjoys herself very much; sometimes I lose, sometimes I win.**"

Mata Hari

executed: put to death

William Stephenson

Stephenson was a Canadian soldier during World War II. He was also a spy for British intelligence. His codename was Intrepid. He passed messages between U.S. President Franklin Roosevelt and British Prime Minister Winston Churchill. He helped change public opinion in the United States about not entering World War II. Fresh troops from the United States turned the tide and helped end the war.

▶ *Stephenson flew into action in World War I after only five hours of flight instruction. He shot down 26 enemy planes and earned the Distinguished Flying Cross medal.*

Ian Fleming based his famous spy, James Bond, on William Stephenson.

SIR WILLIAM STEPHENSON
(1896-1989)
THE MAN CALLED INTREPID

SCULPTOR LEO MOL

The Rosenbergs

Julius and Ethel Rosenberg were American citizens. They were also **communists**. Julius passed sketches of the atom bomb, a devastating weapon, to the Soviets at a time of great tension between the Soviets and Americans. Ethel typed up notes. The pair were caught and convicted of being part of an espionage ring in the United States. Both were executed in Sing Sing Prison in 1953.

XXV ANIV. DEL ASESINATO DE LOS ESPOSOS ROSENBERG

13 CUBA aereo 1978

▲ *In the United States, the Rosenbergs were criminals. But in Cuba, a communist country, they honored them with a stamp.*

communists: people who believe all property should be shared

Animal Spies

Intelligence services don't just depend on people to spy. Sometimes they use animals. Cats, pigeons, ravens, dolphins, and even bats have been trained as spies. Animals are able to get to places where it is too dangerous for humans.

▼ *Dolphins were trained to spot swimmers in restricted waters.*

▲ *In World War II, pigeons were trained to carry messages, maps, and cameras to spy on the enemy.*

Stray or Spy?

Ravens were trained to drop tiles outside of windows. The tiles hid microphones used to tape officials talking. Cats were also given hidden microphones and they wandered in and out of important meetings. Pigeons were trained to point out where soldiers were hiding. When they found one, they landed.

In 2007, the Iranian army captured and held 14 squirrels. They thought they were spying on a **nuclear plant**. The squirrels were later set free when no spy gear was found.

nuclear plant: a place that makes energy from atoms

Mission Impossible

World War I Spies

Most countries used spies before World War I. However, they did not have well-formed spy agencies. World War I changed things. Countries developed new weapons and new battle **tactics**. Spies were very important in finding and bringing back this information.

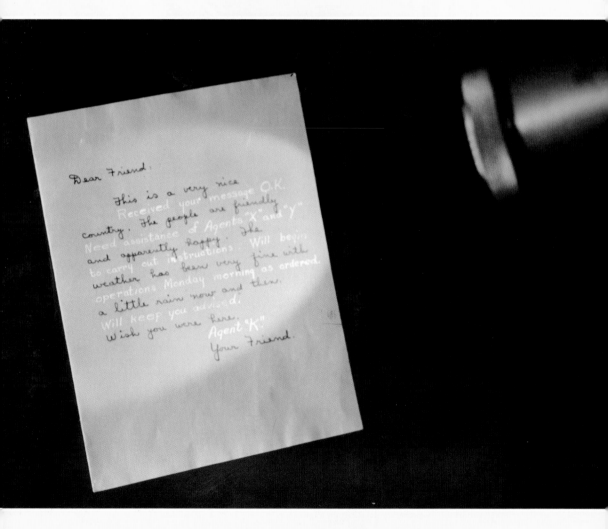

▲ Coded messages using invisible or "disappearing" ink were used in both world wars.

World War II and the Enigma Machine

In World War II, the Germans used a special machine to encode messages. It was called the Enigma machine. Many agents from Britain risked their lives to steal one. They finally got their hands on one after a German U-boat (submarine) was captured. This allowed the British to break the Germans' code and helped win the war.

▼ By capturing the Enigma machine and breaking the code, experts believe World War II was shortened by two years.

Klappe

In Operation Mincemeat, the British planted fake papers on a dead body. The body washed up in Spain. The Germans read that an attack would happen in Greece, but it was really planned for Italy.

tactics: plans of action

The Cold War

After World War II, there was a lot of tension between two **superpower** countries, the United States and the Soviet Union. Different countries took different sides. Both superpowers built up their stockpile of weapons. This period was called the "Cold War" because no direct fighting usually took place.

▲ *In 1962, an American U-2 spy plane discovered the Russians had missile sites set up in communist Cuba. President Kennedy demanded that Soviet leader Khrushchev remove the missiles, which could easily reach the United States. After tense negotiations, the Cuban Missile Crisis ended peacefully.*

Nuclear Weapons

▲ *In 1960, a U-2 spy plane was shot down over the Soviet Union. Photos of military bases were found on board. The United States had to admit they had been spying.*

The Cold War was a war fought with spies and spying. Nuclear technology was new. Each side needed to know what sort of weapons the other side had. They believed that this would keep a balance of power and prevent a full-scale war. The job of collecting that information belonged to spies.

The CIA was able to read the Soviet's coded messages during the Cold War thanks to a mistake by Soviet code clerks in the 1940s. By accident, they reused the same code "key" in different messages. For 40 years, CIA agents used this error to break the code and read secret messages.

superpower: a very powerful country

The Cambridge Five

The Cambridge Five were a ring of spies operating during World War II and into the 1950s. They were British citizens who were unhappy with western **politics**. They became spies for the Soviet Union. They took high-level government jobs. Some even worked for MI6. They fed secrets to the Soviets and cost many lives.

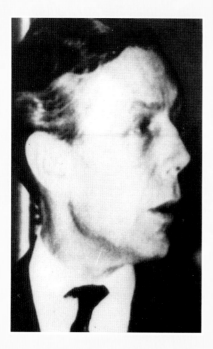

▲ *Anthony Blunt was knighted Sir Anthony Blunt in 1956 but was stripped of his title in 1979 when he was named a spy.*

▲ *Before he could be arrested, Donald Maclean said goodbye to his wife and children and fled to Russia.*

The name of the fifth member of the "Cambridge Five" is still not known. Some believe there were actually more than five members.

Don't Get Caught

Spying during the Cold War was very dangerous. If spies were caught, their governments could not admit they were working for them. It was unlikely that they could be rescued. Often the spies faced prison or death. However, sometimes the two sides exchanged prisoners.

▲ Harold "Kim" Philby worked as a double agent for MI6 and the KGB.

▲ To mask his spying, Guy Burgess spoke badly about communism and joined a pro-Nazi group.

politics: the activities of governments

The Espionage Act

As spying became more common, countries needed to regulate how and when it was done. The Espionage Act was an attempt to do this. In 1917, the U.S. president knew some people did not support the United States entering World War I. He was worried they would try to stop the war effort. They might try to pass secrets to the enemy. On June 15 of that year, this new law made it illegal to spread lies or **interfere** with the military.

During the Cold War, Americans were worried about communists. They believed spies were trying to spread communism in their country. This fear was called the "red scare."

Doing Hard Time

Almost every country has strict laws around spying. Anyone caught spying either in another country or in his or her own country faces prison time or even death. During wartime, countries accept that spies are necessary. However, if they are caught behind enemy lines, they can be executed.

▼ *In the 1950s, Senator Joseph McCarthy believed there were Soviet spies working in the government. His claims were later dismissed, but his accusations ruined the reputations of many innocent citizens.*

interfere: to get in the way of something

Modern Espionage

The job of spying is changing. Computers have made it harder to use a fake identity. Police can access databases around the world that track false passports. Scanning the eye's **iris** is an identification technique used today that is even more accurate than fingerprinting. Spies need to find new ways to hide who they are.

Spies can see what is on your computer screen from far away. They collect the radio waves screens give off. Then a program recreates the images on a new screen.

Web of Spies

The biggest threat today is cyber spying. Online hackers do not only go after governments. They try to get the data from businesses. They want to steal and sell trade secrets. Mining companies are often hacked for the location of gold and gems. Thieves steal credit card numbers and go on spending sprees.

▼ *Cyber spies sometimes use computer viruses. These programs spread to other computers. Spies can then find secret files and pictures from all around the world.*

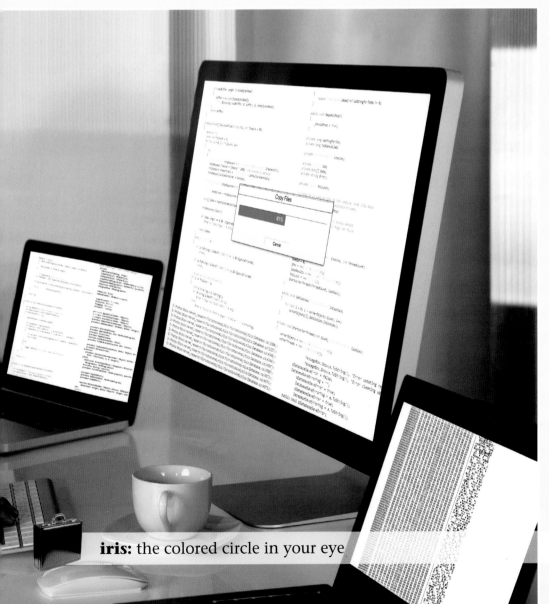

iris: the colored circle in your eye

Whistleblowers

People who spread secrets are called whistleblowers. They want to shame groups into being more open. Their targets are companies and governments. WikiLeaks is a group that posts secret information on the Internet. WikiLeaks has exposed war crimes, abuse of prisoners, and illegal actions by companies. However, many people object to leaking government secrets because it may put the lives of spies and innocent people in danger.

◄ *Julian Assange is the computer hacker and publisher who created WikiLeaks. Currently living in Ecuador's embassy in London, he is protected from facing any charges.*

TIMELINE

1776	1864–65	1909	1914–17
Nathan Hale goes to New York City to gather information on the British.	Elizabeth Van Lew spies for the Union in the Civil War.	Britain creates MI6.	Mata Hari works for German intelligence during World War I.

#StopWatchingUs
www.piratenpartei.de

Who Is Watching You?

American Edward Snowden worked for the CIA and the National Security Agency (NSA). In 2013, he leaked reports about government spying to let the public know what was being "done against them." Some of the spy targets were leaders of other countries. Some were American citizens. He has created a **debate**. Some people say we need to give up some personal privacy to protect our countries. Others say privacy is more important.

◀ *Currently in Russia, Edward Snowden cannot return to the United States without being arrested.*

1917	1936	1942–53
The United States passes the Espionage Act.	William Stephenson begins spying on Hitler for British intelligence.	Julius and Ethel Rosenberg spy for the Soviet Union. They are executed in 1953.

debate: an argument about a particular subject

Books

The Big Book of Spy Stuff
by Bart King
(Gibbs Smith, 2011)

Spies (Horrible Histories
Handbooks)
by Terry Deary
(Scholastic, 2013)

Spies
by Clive Gifford
(Kingfisher, 2004)

Spies (True Crime)
by John Townsend
(Raintree, 2005)

Spy
by Richard Platt
(DK Eyewitness Books, 2009)

*Spy Science: 40 Secret-Sleuthing,
Code-Cracking,
Spy-Catching Activities for Kids*
by Jim Wiese
(Jossey-Bass, 2009)

Websites

www.topspysecrets.com
Learn spy skills and fun spy
crafts

**www.fbi.gov/fun-games/
kids/kids-investigate**
Learn how the FBI investigates

**https://www.cia.gov/kids-
page**
Learn about the CIA

**www.kidzworld.com/
article/7261-becoming-a-
secret-agent**
Discover what it takes to be a
spy

Glossary

classified Very secret and only available to authorized people

communists People who believe all property should be shared

cyber To do with computers

debate An argument about a particular subject

drones Unmanned planes that are controlled from far away

espionage Spying to get information

executed Put to death

exposed Made known to the public

interfere To get in the way of something

iris The colored circle in your eye

microchips Tiny electronic devices that can perform many tasks

mission An important job

nuclear plant A place that makes energy from atoms

officials People with special duties

paralyzed Unable to move all or part of a person's body

politics The activities of governments

restricted Only available to certain people

Soviet Union A former Russian country made up of 15 states

superpower A very powerful country

tactics Plans of action

vital Very necessary

Index

Entries in **bold** refer to pictures